The Life and Passion of St. Cyprian

The Life and Passion of St. Cyprian

St. Cyprian

Life and Passion of St. Cyprian

© Lighthouse Publishing 2023

Written by: St. Cyprian (AD 200 - 258)
Translated by: Rev. Ernest Wallis, Ph.D.(1820 – 1910)
Updated into Modern U.S English: A.M. Overett (b.1960)

All rights reserved. Without limiting the rights under copyright reserved above, no part of this publication may be reproduced, stored in a retrieval system, or transmitted, in any form or by any means (electronic, mechanical, photocopying, recording or otherwise), without the prior written permission of the copyright owner of this book.

Published by
Lighthouse Publishing
SAN 257-4330
228 Freedom Parkway
Hoschton, GA 30548
United States of America

www.lighthousechristianpublishing.com

Introductory Notice to Cyprian.

[a.d. 200–258.]

If Hippolytus reflects the spirit of Irenæus in all his writings, it is not remarkable. He was the spiritual son of the great Bishop of Lyons, and deeply imbued with the family character imparted to his disciples by the blessed presbyter of Patmos and Ephesus. But while Cyprian is the spiritual son and pupil of Tertullian, we must seek his characteristics and the key to his whole ministry in the far-off See and city where the disciples were first called Christians. Cyprian is the Ignatius of the West. We see in his works how truly historical are the writings of Ignatius, and how diffused was his simple and elementary system of organic unity. It embodies no hierarchical assumption, no "lordship over God's heritage," but is conceived in the spirit of St. Peter when he disclaimed all this, and said, "The presbyters who are among you I exhort, who am also a presbyter." Cyprian was indeed a strenuous asserter of the responsibilities of his office; but he built upon that system universally recognized by the Great Councils, which the popes and their adherents have ever labored to destroy. Nothing can be more delusive than the idea that the medieval system derives any support from Cyprian's theory of the episcopate or of Church organization. His was the system of the universal parity and community of bishops. In his scheme the apostolate was perpetuated in the episcopate, and the presbyterate was an apostolic institution, by which others were associated with bishops in all their functions as co-presbyters, but not in those reserved to the presidency of the churches. Feudal ideas imposed a very different system upon the simple framework of original Catholicity. But a careful study of that primitive framework, and of the history of papal development, makes evident the following propositions:—

1. That Cyprian's maxim, Ecclesia in Episcopo, whatever else he may have meant by it, is an aphoristic statement of the Nicene Constitutions. These were embedded in the Ignatian theory of an episcopate without a trace of a papacy; and Cyprian's maxims had to be practically destroyed in the West before it was possible to raise the portentous figure of a supreme pontiff, and to subject the Latin churches to the entirely novel principle of Ecclesia in Papa. To this novelty Cyprian's system is essentially antagonistic.

2. It will be seen that Cyprian, far from being the patron of ecclesiastical despotism, is the expounder of early canons and constitutions, in the spirit of order and discipline, indeed, but with the largest exemplification of that "liberty" which is manifested wherever "the Spirit of the Lord" is operative. Cyprian is the patron and defender of the presbytery and of lay co-operation, as well as of the regimen of the episcopate. His letters illustrate the Catholic system as it was known to the Nicene Fathers; but, of all the Christian Fathers, he is the most clear and comprehensive in his conception of the body of Christ as an organic whole, in which every member has an honorable function. Popular government and representative government, the legitimate power and place of the laity, the organization of the Christian plebs into their faculty as the ἀντιλήψεις of St. Paul, the development of synods, omni plebe adstante,—all this is embodied in the Catholic system as Cyprian understood it.

3. The Orientals in large degree, even under their yoke of bondage and the superstitions engendered by their decay, have ever adhered to this Ignatian theory, of which Cyprian was the great expounder in the West; while the terrible schism of the ninth century, which removed the West from the Nicene basis, and placed the Latin churches upon the foundation of the forged Decretals, was effected by ignoring the Cyprianic maxims, and then by a practical pulverizing of their fundamental principle of unity. This change involved a subversion of the primitive episcopate, an annihilation of the rights of the presbytery, and a total abasement of the laity; in a word, the destruction of synodical constitutions and of constitutional freedom.

4. The constitutional primacy, of which Cyprian was an early promotor, had to be entirely destroyed by decretalism before the papacy could exist. Gregory the Great stood upon the Cyprianic base when he pronounced the author of a scheme for a "universal bishopric" to be a forerunner of Antichrist. It was the spirit of the Decretals to substitute the fictitious idea of a divine supremacy in one bishop and one See, for the canonical presidency of a bishop who was only primus inter pares.

5. Hence the Cyprianic system has ever been the great resource of the "Gallicans against the Ultramontanes" in the cruel but most interesting history of the West. From the Council of Frankfort to our own times Cyprian's spirit is reflected in Hincmar, in Gerbert, in the Gallican canonists, in De Marca, in Bossuet, in Launoy, in Dupin, in Pascal, in the Jansenists (Augustinians), and by the Old Catholics in their late uprising against the dogmatic triumph of Ultramontanism. Nobody can understand the history of Latin Christianity without

mastering the system of Cyprian and comprehending the entirely hostile and uncatholic system of the Decretals.

6. I am not anxious to conceal the fact that I profoundly sympathize with the free spirit, the true benignity, and the moral purity which are everywhere reflected in the writings of Cyprian. If ever American Romanism becomes sufficiently enlightened and purified to comprehend this great Carthaginian Father, and to speak in his tones to the Bishop of Rome, a glorious reformation of this alien religion will be the result; and then we may comprehend the mysterious Providence which has transferred to these shores so many subjects of the despotism of the Vatican. Meanwhile the student of the Ante-Nicene Fathers will not be slow to perceive that he has, in the eight volumes of this series, all that is needful to disarm Romanism, to refute its pretensions, and to direct honest and truth-loving spirits in the Roman Obedience to the door of escape opened by Döllinger and his associates in the "Old Catholic" effort for the restoration of the Latin churches. Let us "speak the truth in love," and pray the Lord to bless this and every endeavor to promote and to sanctify the spirit of enlightened research after the "pattern in the mount." For "thus saith the Lord, Stand ye in the ways, and see and ask for the old paths:" τὰ ἀρχαῖα ἔθη. The following Introduction, from the Edinburgh editor, supplies further answers to inquiry, and suffices to elucidate the subjoined narrative of Pontius.

  Little is known of the early history of Thascius Cyprian (born probably about 200 a.d.) until the period of his intimacy with the Carthaginian presbyter Cæcilius, which led to his conversion a.d. 246. That he was born of respectable parentage, and highly educated for the profession of a rhetorician, is all that can be said with any degree of certainty. At his baptism he assumed the name of his friend Cæcilius, and devoted himself, with all the energies of an ardent and vigorous mind, to the study and practice of Christianity.

His ordination and his elevation to the episcopate rapidly followed his conversion. With some resistance on his own part, and not without great objections on the part of older presbyters, who saw themselves superseded by his promotion, the popular urgency constrained him to accept the office of Bishop of Carthage (a.d. 248), which he held until his martyrdom (a.d. 258).

The writings of Cyprian, apart from their intrinsic worth, have a very considerable historical interest and value, as illustrating the social and religious feelings and usages that then prevailed among the members of the Christian community. Nothing can enable us more vividly to realize the intense convictions—the high-strained enthusiasm—which formed the common level of the Christian experience, than does the indignation with which the prelate denounces the evasions of those who dared not confess, or the lapses of those who shrank from martyrdom. Living in the atmosphere of persecution, and often in the immediate presence of a lingering death, the professors of Christianity were nerved up to a wonderful contempt of suffering and of worldly enjoyment, and saw every event that occurred around them in the glow of their excited imagination; so that many circumstances were sincerely believed and honestly recorded, which will not be for a moment received as true by the calm and critical reader. The account given by Cyprian in his treatise on the Lapsed may serve as an illustration. Of this Dean Milman observes: "In what a high-wrought state of enthusiasm must men have been, who could relate and believe such statements as miraculous!"

Before being advanced to the episcopate, Cyprian had written his Epistle to Donatus shortly after his baptism (a.d. 246); his treatise, or fragment of a treatise, on the Vanity of Idols; and his three books of Testimonies against the Jews. In the following translation the order of Migne has been adopted, which places the letter to Donatus, as seems most natural, first among the Epistles, instead of with the Treatises.

The breaking out of the Decian persecution (a.d. 250) induced Cyprian to retire into concealment for a time; and his retreat gave occasion to a sharp attack upon his conduct, in a letter from the Roman to the Carthaginian clergy. During this year he wrote many letters from his place of concealment to the clergy and others at Rome and at Carthage, controlling, warning, directing, and exhorting, and in every way maintaining his episcopal superintendence in his absence, in all matters connected with the well-being of the Church.

The first 39 of the epistles, excepting the one to Donatus, were probably written during the period of Cyprian's retirement. He appears to have returned to his public duties early in June, 251. Then follow many letters between himself and Cornelius bishop of Rome, and others, on subjects connected with the schisms of Novatian, Novatus, and Felicissimus, and with the condition of those who had been perverted by them. The question proposed in Epistle 52 was settled in the Council that was held in May, 252; and the reference to that anticipated decision limits the date of the letter to about April in the same year. In the 53d Epistle, Cyprian is alluding to the impending persecution of Gallus, under which Cornelius was banished in July, 252. The 56th Epistle was a letter of congratulation to Cornelius on his banishment; and therefore, it must have been written before September 14th in that year, the date of the death of Cornelius. Lucius, his successor, was also banished, and was congratulated on his return by Cyprian in Epistle 57, which therefore must have been written about the end of November, 252. The 59th Epistle is referred by Bishop Pearson to the beginning of the year 253.

There seems nothing to suggest the date of Epistles 60 and 61, except the probability that they were written during a time of peace; and for this reason, they are referred to the beginning of Cyprian's episcopate, before the outbreak of the Decian persecution, a.d. 249. It is usual to assign Epistle 64 to the same year, or at least to a very early period of Cyprian's official life; but it seems scarcely likely that his episcopal counsel should have been sought by a brother bishop in a matter of practice, until he had had some experience; and as it was probably written at a time of peace, when discipline had become relaxed, the date 253 seems preferable. The 68th Epistle is easily dated by the reference, on page 246, to an episcopate of six years' duration; and it must therefore have been written in a.d. 254. On the 14th September, Cyprian was banished to Curubis by the Emperor Valerian. From his place of exile, he wrote Epistle 76, which was replied to in Epistles 77, 78, and 79. Doubts are entertained as to the date of Epistle 80, whether it should be referred to a.d. 250 or 257. Pamelius prefers the latter date, on the ground that the Rogatianus to whom it is inscribed was one who survived the Decian persecution, and a younger man than the one who, as he supposes, was declared to have suffered martyrdom at the date of this Epistle. This, however, seems very unsatisfactory; and the weight of authority is in favor of the earlier date. The remaining Epistles are easily limited by their contents to the period immediately preceding Cyprian's martyrdom.

For the sake of uniformity, it has been thought well to adhere to the arrangement of Migne, in the order of the Epistles as well as in their divisions. For the convenience of reference, however, the number of each Epistle in the Oxford edition is appended in a note. For a similar reason, the general form of Migne's text has been used in the following translation; but the use of other texts and of preceding translations has not been rejected in the endeavor to approximate to the sense of the author. Moreover, such various readings as might suggest different shades of meaning in doubtful passages have been given.

The Translator has only to add, that, as a rule, an exact rendering has been sought after, sometimes in preference to a version in fluent English. But, except in cases where the corruption or obscurity of the text seems insurmountable, the meaning of the writer is believed to be given fairly and intelligibly. The style of Cyprian, like that of his master Tertullian, is marked much more by vehemence than perspicuity, and it is often no easy matter to give exact expression in another language to the idea contained in the original text. Cyprian's Life, as written by his own deacon Pontius, is subjoined.

Note by the American Editor. It is easy to speak with ridicule of such instances as Dean Milman here treats so philosophically. But, lest believers should be charged with exceptional credulity, let us recall what the father of English Deism relates of his own experiences, in the conclusion of his Autobiography: "I had no sooner spoken these words (of prayer to the Deist's deity) but a loud though yet a gentle noise came from the heavens, for it was like nothing on earth, which did so comfort and cheer me, that I took my petition as granted, and that I had the sign I demanded....This, how strange soever it may seem, I protest, before the eternal God, is true," etc. Life of Herbert, p. 52, Popular Authors(no date). London. From Horace Walpole's edition.

The Life and Passion of Cyprian, Bishop and Martyr. By Pontius the Deacon.

---

1. Although Cyprian, the devout priest and glorious witness of God, composed many writings whereby the memory of his worthy name survives; and although the profuse fertility of his eloquence and of God's grace so expands itself in the exuberance and richness of his discourse, that he will probably never cease to speak even to the end of the world; yet, since to his works and deserts it is justly due that his example should be recorded in writing, I have thought it well to prepare this brief and compendious narrative. Not that the life of so great a man can be unknown to any even of the heathen nations, but that to our posterity also this incomparable and lofty pattern may be prolonged into immortal remembrance. It would assuredly be hard that, when our fathers have given such honor even to lay-

people and catechumens who have obtained martyrdom, for reverence of their very martyrdom, as to record many, or I had nearly said, well-nigh all, of the circumstances of their sufferings, so that they might be brought to our knowledge also who as yet were not born, the passion of such a priest and such a martyr as Cyprian should be passed over, who, independently of his martyrdom, had much to teach, and that what he did while he lived should be hidden from the world. And, indeed, these doings of his were such, and so great, and so admirable, that I am deterred by the contemplation of their greatness, and confess myself incompetent to discourse in a way that shall be worthy of the honor of his deserts, and unable to relate such noble deeds in such a way that they may appear as great as in fact they are, except that the multitude of his glories is itself sufficient for itself, and needs no other heraldry. It enhances my difficulty, that you also are anxious to hear very much, or if it be possible everything, about him, longing with eager warmth at least to become acquainted with his deeds, although now his living words are silent. And in this behalf, if I should say that the powers of eloquence fail me, I should say too little. For eloquence itself fails of suitable powers fully to satisfy your desire. And thus, I am sorely pressed on both sides, since he burdens me with his virtues, and you press me hard with your entreaties.

2. At what point, then, shall I begin,—from what direction shall I approach the description of his goodness, except from the beginning of his faith and from his heavenly birth? inasmuch as the doings of a man of God should not be reckoned from any point except from the time that he was born of God. He may have had pursuits previously, and liberal arts may have imbued his mind

while engaged therein; but these things I pass over; for as yet they had nothing to do with anything but his secular advantage. But when he had learned sacred knowledge, and breaking through the clouds of this world had emerged into the light of spiritual wisdom, if I was with him in any of his doings, if I have discerned any of his more illustrious labors, I will speak of them; only asking meanwhile for this indulgence, that whatever I shall say too little (for too little I must needs say) may rather be attributed to my ignorance than subtracted from his glory. While his faith was in its first rudiments, he believed that before God nothing was worthy in comparison of the observance of continency. For he thought that the heart might then become what it ought to be, and the mind attain to the full capacity of truth, if he trod underfoot the lust of the flesh with the robust and healthy vigor of holiness. Who has ever recorded such a marvel? His second birth had not yet enlightened the new man with the entire splendor of the divine light, yet he was already overcoming the ancient and pristine darkness by the mere dawning of the light. Then—what is even greater—when he had learned from the reading of Scripture certain things not according to the condition of his novitiate, but in proportion to the earliness of his faith, he immediately laid hold of what he had discovered, for his own advantage in deserving well of God. By distributing his means for the relief of the indigence of the poor, by dispensing the purchase-money of entire estates, he at once realized two benefits,—the contempt of this world's ambition, than which nothing is more pernicious, and the observance of that mercy which God has preferred even to His sacrifices, and which even he did not maintain who said that he had kept all the commandments of the law;

whereby with premature swiftness of piety he almost began to be perfect before he had learnt the way to be perfect. Who of the ancients, I pray, has done this? Who of the most celebrated veterans in the faith, whose hearts and ears have throbbed to the divine words for many years, has attempted any such thing, as this man—of faith yet unskilled, and whom, perhaps, as yet nobody trusted—surpassing the age of antiquity, accomplished by his glorious and admirable labors? No one reaps immediately upon his sowing; no one presses out the vintage harvest from the trenches just formed; no one ever yet sought for ripened fruit from newly planted slips. But in him all incredible things concurred. In him the threshing preceded (if it may be said, for the thing is beyond belief)—preceded the sowing, the vintage the shoots, the fruit the root.

3. The apostle's epistle says that novices should be passed over, lest by the stupor of heathenism that yet clings to their unconfirmed minds, their untaught inexperience should in any respect sin against God. He first, and I think he alone, furnished an illustration that greater progress is made by faith than by time. For although in the Acts of the Apostles the eunuch is described as at once baptized by Philip, because he believed with his whole heart, this is not a fair parallel. For he was a Jew, and as he came from the temple of the Lord he was reading the prophet Isaiah, and he hoped in Christ, although as yet he did not believe that He had come; while the other, coming from the ignorant heathens, began with a faith as mature as that with which few perhaps have finished their course. In short, in respect of God's grace, there was no delay, no postponement,—I have said but little,—he immediately

received the presbyterate and the priesthood. For who is there that would not entrust every grade of honor to one who believed with such a disposition? There are many things which he did while still a layman, and many things which now as a presbyter he did—many things which, after the examples of righteous men of old, and following them with a close imitation, he accomplished with the obedience of entire consecration—that deserved well of the Lord. For his discourse concerning this was usually, that if he had read of any one being set forth with the praise of God, he would persuade us to inquire on account of what doings he had pleased God. If Job, glorious by God's testimony, was called a true worshipper of God, and one to whom there was none upon earth to be compared, he taught that we should do whatever Job had previously done, so that while we are doing like things we may call forth a similar testimony of God for ourselves. He, contemning the loss of his estate, gained such advantage by his virtue thus tried, that he had no perception of the temporal losses even of his affection. Neither poverty nor pain broke him down; the persuasion of his wife did not influence him; the dreadful suffering of his own body did not shake his firmness. His virtue remained established in its own home, and his devotion, founded upon deep roots, gave way under no onset of the devil tempting him to abstain from blessing his God with a grateful faith even in his adversity. His house was open to every comer. No widow returned from him with an empty lap; no blind man was unguided by him as a companion; none faltering in step was unsupported by him for a staff; none stripped of help by the hand of the mighty was not protected by him as a defender. Such things ought they to do, he was accustomed to say, who desire to please God. And thus, running through the examples of all good men, by always imitating those who were better than others he made himself also worthy of imitation.

4. He had a close association among us with a just man, and of praiseworthy memory, by name Cæcilius, and in age as well as in honor a presbyter, who had converted him from his worldly errors to the acknowledgment of the true divinity. This man he loved with entire honor and all observance, regarding him with an obedient veneration, not only as the friend and comrade of his soul, but as the parent of his new life. And at length he, influenced by his attentions, was, as well he might be, stimulated to such a pitch of excessive love, that when he was departing from this world, and his summons was at hand, he commended to him his wife and children; so that him whom he had made a partner in the fellowship of his way of life, he afterwards made the heir of his affection.

5. It would be tedious to go through individual circumstances, it would be laborious to enumerate all his doings. For the proof of his good works I think that this one thing is enough, that by the judgment of God and the favor of the people, he was chosen to the office of the priesthood and the degree of the episcopate while still a neophyte, and, as it was considered, a novice. Although still in the early days of his faith, and in the untaught season of his spiritual life, a generous disposition so shone forth in him, that although not yet resplendent with the glitter of office, but only of hope, he gave promise of entire trust worthiness for the priesthood that was coming upon him. Moreover, I will not pass over that remarkable fact, of the way in which, when the entire

people by God's inspiration leapt forward in his love and honor, he humbly withdrew, giving place to men of older standing, and thinking himself unworthy of a claim to so great honor, so that he thus became more worthy. For he is made more worthy who dispenses with what he deserves. And with this excitement were the eager people at that time inflamed, desiring with a spiritual longing, as the event proved, not only a bishop,—for in him whom then with a latent foreboding of divinity they were in such wise demanding, they were seeking not only a priest,— but moreover a future martyr. A crowded fraternity was besieging the doors of the house, and throughout all the avenues of access an anxious love was circulating. Possibly that apostolic experience might then have happened to him, as he desired, of being let down through a window, had he also been equal to the apostle in the honor of ordination. It was plain to be seen that all the rest were expecting his coming with an anxious spirit of suspense, and received him when he came with excessive joy. I speak unwillingly, but I must needs speak. Some resisted him, even that he might overcome them; yet with what gentleness, how patiently, how benevolently he gave them indulgence! how mercifully he forgave them, reckoning them afterwards, to the astonishment of many, among his closest and, most intimate friends! For who would not be amazed at the forgetfulness of a mind so retentive?

6. Henceforth who is sufficient to relate the manner in which he bore himself?—what pity was his? what vigor? how great his mercy? how great his strictness? So much sanctity and grace beamed from his face that it confounded the minds of the beholders. His countenance was grave and joyous. Neither was his

severity gloomy, nor his affability excessive, but a mingled tempering of both; so that it might be doubted whether he most deserved to be revered or to be loved, except that he deserved both to be revered and to be loved. And his dress was not out of harmony with his countenance, being itself also subdued to a fitting mean. The pride of the world did not inflame him, nor yet did an excessively affected penury make him sordid, because this latter kind of attire arises no less from boastfulness, than does such an ambitious frugality from ostentation. But what did he as bishop in respect of the poor, whom as a catechumen he had loved? Let the priests of piety consider, or those whom the teaching of their very rank has trained to the duty of good works, or those whom the common obligation of the Sacrament has bound to the duty of manifesting love. Cyprian the bishop's cathedra received such as he had been before,—it did not make him so.

7. And therefore for such merits he at once obtained the glory of proscription also. For nothing else was proper than that he who in the secret recesses of his conscience was rich in the full honor of religion and faith, should moreover be renowned in the publicly diffused report of the Gentiles. He might, indeed, at that time, in accordance with the rapidity wherewith he always attained everything, have hastened to the crown of martyrdom appointed for him, especially when with repeated calls he was frequently demanded for the lions, had it not been needful for him to pass through all the grades of glory, and thus to arrive at the highest, and had not the impending desolation needed the aid of so fertile a mind. For conceive of him as being at that time taken away by the dignity of martyrdom. Who was there to

show the advantage of grace, advancing by faith? Who was there to restrain virgins to the fitting discipline of modesty and a dress worthy of holiness, as if with a kind of bridle of the lessons of the Lord? Who was there to teach penitence to the lapsed, truth to heretics, unity to schismatics, peacefulness and the law of evangelical prayer to the sons of God? By whom were the blaspheming Gentiles to be overcome by retorting upon themselves the accusations which they heap upon us? By whom were Christians of too tender an affection, or, what is of more importance, of a too feeble faith in respect of the loss of their friends, to be consoled with the hope of futurity? Whence should we so learn mercy? whence patience? Who was there to restrain the ill blood arising from the envenomed malignity of envy, with the sweetness of a wholesome remedy? Who was there to raise up such great martyrs by the exhortation of his divine discourse? Who was there, in short, to animate so many confessors sealed with a second inscription on their distinguished brows, and reserved alive for an example of martyrdom, kindling their ardor with a heavenly trumpet? Fortunately, fortunately it occurred then, and truly by the Spirit's direction, that the man who was needed for so many and so excellent purposes was withheld from the consummation of martyrdom. Do you wish to be assured that the cause of his withdrawal was not fear? to allege nothing else, he did suffer subsequently, and this suffering he assuredly would have evaded as usual, if he had evaded it before. It was indeed that fear—and rightly so—that fear which would dread to offend the Lord—that fear which prefers to obey God's commands rather than to be crowned in disobedience. For a mind dedicated in all things to God, and thus enslaved to the divine admonitions, believed that even in suffering itself it would sin, unless it had obeyed the Lord, who then bade him seek the place of concealment.

8. Moreover, I think that something may here be said about the benefit of the delay, although I have already touched slightly on the matter. By what appears subsequently to have occurred, it follows that we may prove that that withdrawal was not conceived by human pusillanimity, but, as indeed is the case, was truly divine. The unusual and violent rage of a cruel persecution had laid waste God's people; and since the artful enemy could not deceive all by one fraud, wherever the incautious soldier laid bare his side, there in various manifestations of rage he had destroyed individuals with different kinds of overthrow. There needed someone who could, when men were wounded and hurt by the various arts of the attacking enemy, use the remedy of the celestial medicine according to the nature of the wound, either for cutting or for cherishing them. Thus was preserved a man of an intelligence, besides other excellences, also spiritually trained, who between the resounding waves of the opposing schisms could steer the middle course of the Church in a steady path. Are not such plans, I ask, divine? Could this have been done without God? Let them consider who think that such things as these can happen by chance. To them the Church replies with clear voice, saying, "I do not allow and do not believe that such needful then are reserved without the decree of God."

9. Still, if it seem well, let me glance at the rest. Afterwards there broke out a dreadful plague, and excessive destruction of a hateful disease invaded every house in succession of the trembling populace, carrying off day by day with abrupt attack numberless people,

everyone from his own house. All were shuddering, fleeing, shunning the contagion, impiously exposing their own friends, as if with the exclusion of the person who was sure to die of the plague, one could exclude death itself also. There lay about the meanwhile, over the whole city, no longer bodies, but the carcasses of many, and, by the contemplation of a lot which in their turn would be theirs, demanded the pity of the passers-by for themselves. No one regarded anything besides his cruel gains. No one trembled at the remembrance of a similar event. No one did to another what he himself wished to experience. In these circumstances, it would be a wrong to pass over what the pontiff of Christ did, who excelled the pontiffs of the world as much in kindly affection as he did in truth of religion. On the people assembled together in one place he first of all urged the benefits of mercy, teaching by examples from divine lessons, how greatly the duties of benevolence avail to deserve well of God. Then afterwards he subjoined, that there was nothing wonderful in our cherishing our own people only with the needed attentions of love, but that he might become perfect who would do something more than the publican or the heathen, who, overcoming evil with good, and practicing a clemency which was like the divine clemency, loved even his enemies, who would pray for the salvation of those that persecute him, as the Lord admonishes and exhorts. God continually makes His sun to rise, and from time to time gives showers to nourish the seed, exhibiting all these kindnesses not only to His people, but to aliens also. And if a man professes to be a son of God, why does not he imitate the example of his Father? "It becomes us," said he, "to answer to our birth; and it is not fitting that those who are evidently born of

God should be degenerate, but rather that the propagation of a good Father should be proved in His offspring by the emulation of His goodness."

10. I omit many other matters, and, indeed, many important ones, which the necessity of a limited space does not permit to be detailed in more lengthened discourse, and concerning which this much is sufficient to have been said. But if the Gentiles could have heard these things as they stood before the rostrum, they would probably at once have believed. What, then, should a Christian people do, whose very name proceeds from faith? Thus the ministrations are constantly distributed according to the quality of the men and their degrees. Many who, by the straitness of poverty, were unable to manifest the kindness of wealth, manifested more than wealth, making up by their own labor a service dearer than all riches. And under such a teacher, who would not press forward to be found in some part of such a warfare, whereby he might please both God the Father, and Christ the Judge, and for the present so excellent a priest? Thus what is good was done in the liberality of overflowing works to all men, not to those only who are of the household of faith. Something more was done than is recorded of the incomparable benevolence of Tobias. He must forgive, and forgive again, and frequently forgive; or, to speak more truly, he must of right concede that, although very much might be done before Christ, yet that something more might be done after Christ, since to His times all fulness is attributed. Tobias collected together those who were slain by the king and cast out, of his own race only.

11. Banishment followed these actions, so good and so benevolent. For impiety always makes this return,

that it repays the better with the worse. And what God's priest replied to the interrogation of the proconsul, there are Acts which relate. In the meantime, he is excluded from the city who had done some good for the city's safety; he who had striven that the eyes of the living should not suffer the horrors of the infernal abode; he, I say, who, vigilant in the watches of benevolence, had provided—oh wickedness! with unacknowledged goodness—that when all were forsaking the desolate appearance of the city, a destitute state and a deserted country should not perceive its many exiles. But let the world look to this, which accounts banishment a penalty. To them, their country is too dear, and they have the same name as their parents; but we abhor even our parents themselves if they would persuade us against God. To them, it is a severe punishment to live outside their own city; to the Christian, the whole of this world is one home. Wherefore, though he were banished into a hidden and secret place, yet, associated with the affairs of his God, he cannot regard it as an exile. In addition, while honestly serving God, he is a stranger even in his own city. For while the continency of the Holy Spirit restrains him from carnal desires, he lays aside the conversation of the former man, and even among his fellow-citizens, or, I might almost say, among the parents themselves of his earthly life, he is a stranger. Besides, although this might otherwise appear to be a punishment, yet in causes and sentences of this kind, which we suffer for the trial of the proof of our virtue, it is not a punishment, because it is a glory. But, indeed, suppose banishment not to be a punishment to us, yet the witness of their own conscience may still attribute the last and worst wickedness to those who can lay upon the innocent what they think to be a punishment. I will not now describe a charming place; and, for the present, I pass over the addition of all possible delights. Let us conceive of the place, filthy in situation, squalid in appearance, having no wholesome water, no pleasantness of verdure, no neighboring shore, but vast wooded rocks between the inhospitable jaws of a totally deserted solitude, far removed in the pathless regions of the world. Such a place might have borne the name of exile, if Cyprian, the priest of God, had come thither; although to him, if the ministrations of men had been wanting, either birds, as in the case of Elias, or angels, as in that of Daniel, would have ministered. Away, away with the belief that anything would be wanting to the least of us, so long as he stands for the confession of the name. So far was God's pontiff, who had always been urgent in merciful works, from needing the assistance of all these things.

12. And now let us return with thankfulness to what I had suggested in the second place, that for the soul of such a man there was divinely provided a sunny and suitable spot, a dwelling, secret as he wished, and all that has before been promised to be added to those who seek the kingdom and righteousness of God. And, not to mention the number of the brethren who visited him, and then the kindness of the citizens themselves, which supplied to him everything whereof he appeared to be deprived, I will not pass over God's wonderful visitation, whereby He wished His priest in exile to be so certain of his passion that was to follow, that in his full confidence of the threatening martyrdom, Curubis possessed not only an exile, but a martyr too. For on that day whereon we first abode in the place of banishment (for the condescension of his love had chosen me among his

household companions to a voluntary exile: would that he could also have chosen me to share his passion!), "there appeared to me," said he, "ere yet I was sunk in the repose of slumber, a young man of unusual stature, who, as it were, led me to the prætorium, where I seemed to myself to be led before the tribunal of the proconsul, then sitting. When he looked upon me, he began at once to note down a sentence on his tablet, which I knew not, for he had asked nothing of me with the accustomed interrogation. But the youth, who was standing at his back, very anxiously read what had been noted down. And because he could not then declare it in words, he showed me by an intelligible sign what was contained in the writing of that tablet. For, with hand expanded and flattened like a blade, he imitated the stroke of the accustomed punishment, and expressed what he wished to be understood as clearly as by speech,—I understood the future sentence of my passion. I began to ask and to beg immediately that a delay of at least one day should be accorded me, until I should have arranged my property in some reasonable order. And when I had urgently repeated my entreaty, he began again to note down, I know not what, on his tablet. But I perceived from the calmness of his countenance that the judge's mind was moved by my petition, as being a just one. Moreover, that youth, who already had disclosed to me the intelligence of my passion by gesture rather than by words, hastened to signify repeatedly by secret signal that the delay was granted which had been asked for until the morrow, twisting his fingers one behind the other. And I, although the sentence had not been read, although I rejoiced with very glad heart with joy at the delay accorded, yet trembled so with fear of the uncertainty of the interpretation, that the remains of fear still set my exulting heart beating with excessive agitation."

13. What could be plainer than this revelation? What could be more blessed than this condescension? Everything was foretold to him beforehand which subsequently followed. Nothing was diminished of the words of God, nothing was mutilated of so sacred a promise. Carefully consider each particular in accordance with its announcement. He asks for delay till the morrow, when the sentence of his passion was under deliberation, begging that he might arrange his affairs on the day which he had thus obtained. This one day signified a year, which he was about to pass in the world after his vision. For, to speak more plainly, after the year was expired, he was crowned, on that day on which, at the commencement of the year, the fact had been announced to him. For although we do not read of the day of the Lord as a year in sacred Scripture, yet we regard that space of time as due in making promise of future things. Whence is it of no consequence if, in this case, under the ordinary expression of a day, it is only a year that in this place is implied, because that which is the greater ought to be fuller in meaning. Moreover, that it was explained rather by signs than by speech, was because the utterance of speech was reserved for the manifestation of the time itself. For anything is usually set forth in words, whenever what is set forth is accomplished. For, indeed, no one knew why this had been shown to him, until afterwards, when, on the very day on which he had seen it, he was crowned. Nevertheless, in the meantime, his impending suffering was certainly known by all, but the exact day of his passion was not spoken of by any of the same, just as if they were ignorant of it. And, indeed, I find something

similar in the Scriptures. For Zacharias the priest, because he did not believe the promise of a son, made to him by the angel, became dumb; so that he asked for tablets by a sign, being about to write his son's name rather than utter it. With reason, also in this case, where God's messenger declared the impending passion of His priest rather by signs, he both admonished his faith and fortified His priest. Moreover, the ground of asking for delay arose out of his wish to arrange his affairs and settle his will. Yet what affairs or what will had he to arrange, except ecclesiastical concerns? And thus that last delay was received, in order that whatever had to be disposed of by his final decision concerning the care of cherishing the poor might be arranged. And I think that for no other reason, and indeed for this reason only, indulgence was granted to him even by those very persons who had ejected and were about to slay him, that, being at hand, he might relieve the poor also who were before him with the final or, to speak more accurately, with the entire outlay of his last stewardship. And therefore, having so benevolently ordered matters, and so arranged them according to his will, the morrow drew near.

14. Now also a messenger came to him from the city from Xistus, the good and peace-making priest, and on that account most blessed martyr. The coming executioner was instantly looked for who should strike through that devoted neck of the most sacred victim; and thus, in the daily expectation of dying, every day was to him as if the crown might be attributed to each. In the meantime, there assembled to him many eminent people, and people of most illustrious rank and family, and noble with the world's distinctions, who, on account of ancient friendship with him, repeatedly urged his withdrawal;

and, that their urgency might not be in some sort hollow, they also offered places to which he might retire. But he had now set the world aside, having his mind suspended upon heaven, and did not consent to their tempting persuasions. He would perhaps even then have done what was asked for by so many and faithful friends, if it had been bidden him by divine command. But that lofty glory of so great a man must not be passed over without announcement, that now, when the world was swelling, and of its trust in its princes breathing out hatred of the name, he was instructing God's servants, as opportunity was given, in the exhortations of the Lord, and was animating them to tread underfoot the sufferings of this present time by the contemplation of a glory to come hereafter. Indeed, such was his love of sacred discourse, that he wished that his prayers in regard to his suffering might be so answered, that he would be put to death in the very act of speaking about God.

15. And these were the daily acts of a priest destined for a pleasing sacrifice to God, when, behold, at the bidding of the proconsul, the officer with his soldiers on a sudden came unexpectedly on him,—or rather, to speak more truly, thought that he had come unexpectedly on him, at his gardens,—at his gardens, I say, which at the beginning of his faith he had sold, and which, being restored by God's mercy, he would assuredly have sold again for the use of the poor, if he had not wished to avoid ill-will from the persecutors. But when could a mind ever prepared be taken unawares, as if by an unforeseen attack? Therefore now he went forward, certain that what had been long delayed would be settled. He went forward with a lofty and elevated mien, manifesting cheerfulness in his look and courage in his heart. But being delayed to

the morrow, he returned from the praetorium to the officer's house, when on a sudden a scattered rumor prevailed throughout all Carthage, that now Thascius was brought forward, whom there was nobody who did not know as well for his illustrious fame in the honorable opinion of all, as on account of the recollection of his most renowned work. On all sides all men were flocking together to a spectacle, to us glorious from the devotion of faith, and to be mourned over even by the Gentiles. A gentle custody, however, had him in charge when taken and placed for one night in the officer's house; so that we, his associates and friends, were as usual in his company. The whole people in the meantime, in anxiety that nothing should be done throughout the night without their knowledge, kept watch before the officer's door. The goodness of God granted him at that time, so truly worthy of it, that even God's people should watch on the passion of the priest. Yet, perhaps, someone may ask what was the reason of his returning from the praetorium to the officer. And some think that this arose from the fact, that for his own part the proconsul was then unwilling. Far be it from me to complain, in matters divinely ordered, of slothfulness or aversion in the proconsul. Far be it from me to admit such an evil into the consciousness of a religious mind, as that the fancy of man should decide the fate of so blessed a martyr. But the morrow, which a year before the divine condescension had foretold, required to be literally the morrow.

16. At last that other day dawned—that destined, that promised, that divine day—which, if even the tyrant himself had wished to put off, he would not have had any power to do so; the day rejoicing at the consciousness of the future martyr; and, the clouds being scattered

throughout the circuit of the world, the day shone upon them with a brilliant sun. He went out from the house of the officer, though he was the officer of Christ and God, and was walled in on all sides by the ranks of a mingled multitude. And such a numberless army hung upon his company, as if they had come with an assembled troop to assault death itself. Now, as he went, he had to pass by the racecourse. And rightly, and as if it had been contrived on purpose, he had to pass by the place of a corresponding struggle, who, having finished his contest, was running to the crown of righteousness. But when he had come to the praetorium, as the proconsul had not yet come forth, a place of retirement was accorded him. There, as he sat moistened after his long journey with excessive perspiration (the seat was by chance covered with linen, so that even in the very moment of his passion he might enjoy the honor of the episcopate), one of the officers ("Tesserarius"), who had formerly been a Christian, offered him his clothes, as if he might wish to change his moistened garments for drier ones; and he doubtless coveted nothing further in respect of his proffered kindness than to possess the now blood-stained sweat of the martyr going to God. He made reply to him, and said, "We apply medicines to annoyances which probably to-day will no longer exist." Is it any wonder that he despised suffering in body who had despised death in soul? Why should we say more? He was suddenly announced to the proconsul; he is brought forward; he is placed before him; he is interrogated as to his name. He answers who he is, and nothing more.

17. And thus, therefore, the judge reads from his tablet the sentence which lately in the vision he had not read,—a spiritual sentence, not rashly to be spoken,—a

sentence worthy of such a bishop and such a witness; a glorious sentence, wherein he was called a standard-bearer of the sect, and an enemy of the gods, and one who was to be an example to his people; and that with his blood discipline would begin to be established. Nothing could be more complete, nothing more true, than this sentence. For all the things which were said, although said by a heathen, are divine. Nor is it indeed to be wondered at, since priests are accustomed to prophesy of the passion. He had been a standard-bearer, who was accustomed to teach concerning the bearing of Christ's standard; he had been an enemy of the gods, who commanded the idols to be destroyed. Moreover, he gave example to his friends, since, when many were about to follow in a similar manner, he was the first in the province to consecrate the first-fruits of martyrdom. And by his blood discipline began to be established; but it was the discipline of martyrs, who, emulating their teacher, in the imitation of a glory like his own, themselves also gave a confirmation to discipline by the very blood of their own example.

18. And when he left the doors of the praetorium, a crowd of soldiery accompanied him; and that nothing might be wanting in his passion, centurions and tribunes guarded his side. Now the place itself where he was about to suffer is level, so that it affords a noble spectacle, with its trees thickly planted on all sides. But as, by the extent of the space beyond, the view was not attainable to the confused crowd, persons who favored him had climbed up into the branches of the trees, that there might not even be wanting to him (what happened in the case of Zacchæus), that he was gazed upon from the trees. And now, having with his own hands bound his eyes, he tried

to hasten the slowness of the executioner, whose office was to wield the sword, and who with difficulty clasped the blade in his failing right hand with trembling fingers, until the mature hour of glorification strengthened the hand of the centurion with power granted from above to accomplish the death of the excellent man, and at length supplied him with the permitted strength. O blessed people of the Church, who as well in sight as in feeling, and, what is more, in outspoken words, suffered with such a bishop as theirs; and, as they had ever heard him in his own discourses, were crowned by God the Judge! For although that which the general wish desired could not occur, viz., that the entire congregation should suffer at once in the fellowship of a like glory, yet whoever under the eyes of Christ beholding, and in the hearing of the priest, eagerly desired to suffer, by the sufficient testimony of that desire did in some sort send a missive to God, as his ambassador.

19. His passion being thus accomplished, it resulted that Cyprian, who had been an example to all good men, was also the first who in Africa imbued his priestly crown with blood of martyrdom, because he was the first who began to be such after the apostles. For from the time at which the episcopal order is enumerated at Carthage, not one is ever recorded, even of good men and priests, to have come to suffering. Although devotion surrendered to God is always in consecrated men reckoned instead of martyrdom; yet Cyprian attained even to the perfect crown by the consummation of the Lord; so that in that very city in which he had in such wise lived, and in which he had been the first to do many noble deeds, he also was the first to decorate the insignia of his heavenly priesthood with glorious gore. What shall I do

now? Between joy at his passion, and grief at still remaining, my mind is divided in different directions, and twofold affections are burdening a heart too limited for them. Shall I grieve that I was not his associate? But yet I must triumph in his victory. Shall I triumph at his victory? Still I grieve that I am not his companion. Yet still to you I must in simplicity confess, what you also are aware of, that it was my intention to be his companion. Much and excessively I exult at his glory; but still more do I grieve that I remained behind.

Find this and other great works of the early Church Fathers at lighthousechristianpublishing.com.

St. Cyprian

Our Father who art in heaven, hallowed be
thy name.
Thy kingdom come, Thy will be done, on
earth as it is in heaven.
Give us this day our daily bread and
forgive us our trespasses as we forgive those who
trespass against us.
And lead us not into temptation, but deliver
us from evil, for Thy is the kingdom, the power
and the glory.

Amen

Hail Mary full of grace, the Lord is with thee. Blessed art thou amongst women and blessed is the fruit of thy womb Jesus. Holy Mary mother of God, pray for us sinners, now and the hour of our death.

www.ingramcontent.com/pod-product-compliance
Lightning Source LLC
Chambersburg PA
CBHW071256070526
44583CB00017B/2489